"The wind as an energy source: From history to the future"

"Wings of Change: Wind Energy Through the Ages"

Table of contents

introduction

1.1 Why wind turbines are important

1.2 Aim and structure of the book

Chapter 1: The History of Wind Power

1.1 The beginnings of wind energy use

1.2 Development of modern wind power technology

1.3 Milestones in the history of wind power

Conclusion

12.1 Summary of key findings

12.2 Outlook on the role of wind power in the future

Attachment

A. Glossary of technical terms

introduction

1.1 Why wind turbines are important

Wind turbines are important for various reasons:

Renewable energy source: Wind turbines produce clean, renewable energy by converting the kinetic energy of the wind into electrical energy. This reduces dependence on fossil fuels such as coal, oil and natural gas, which contribute to air pollution and the greenhouse effect.

Reducing greenhouse gas emissions: The use of wind energy helps reduce emissions of greenhouse gases, particularly carbon dioxide (CO2). With climate change one of the most pressing global challenges, switching to clean energy sources such as wind power is crucial.

Reducing air pollution: Wind energy production produces no air pollution compared to fossil fuels, improving air quality and promoting population health.

Energy independence: Wind energy can be generated locally, strengthening a country's energy independence and reducing vulnerability to fossil fuel price fluctuations.

Job creation: The installation, maintenance and manufacturing of wind turbines creates jobs and promotes economic growth in the region.

Technological development: The development of wind power technologies has made significant progress in recent years. This has not only improved the efficiency of the systems, but also promoted innovations in energy technology.

Sustainable energy source: Wind is a sustainable energy source because it is inexhaustible and does not have harmful effects on the environment such as fossil fuel extraction.

Contribution to the energy transition: Wind energy is an important part of the energy transition, which aims to shift energy production towards environmentally friendly, sustainable sources and reduce CO2 emissions.

Power supply and grid stability: Wind turbines can contribute to power supply and improve grid stability, especially when combined with other renewable energy sources such as solar energy and energy storage technologies.

Long-term cost savings: Although the initial investment in wind turbines can be high, the long-term operating costs are comparatively low. This can lead to cost savings in the long term.

Overall, wind turbines are important for meeting global energy needs, combating climate change, protecting the environment and creating a sustainable energy future.

Chapter 1: The History of Wind Power

1.1 The beginnings of wind energy use

The use of wind energy has a long history, dating back to ancient times. Here are some important milestones in the development of wind energy use:

Ancient Windmills: The oldest known windmills were used in Persia (modern-day Iran) in the 7th century AD. These early windmills were primarily used to irrigate fields.

European Windmills: Windmills spread throughout Europe in the Middle Ages. Particularly in the Netherlands and what is now Germany, windmills were used for a variety of purposes, including grinding grain and pumping water.

Wind Pumps in North America: In the 19th century, wind pumps were widely used in the United States to pump water for agriculture. These wind pumps helped cultivate dry areas.

Electric Power Generation: The breakthrough in the use of wind energy to generate electricity occurred in the late 19th and early 20th centuries. The first wind turbine to generate electricity was built in Denmark in 1891. However, this turbine has not yet had a major impact on the electricity supply.

Further development of wind turbines: In the following decades, wind turbines became technologically more developed and became more efficient. In the 1980s and 1990s, modern wind turbines with aerodynamic rotor blades and powerful generators began to appear.

Wind Energy Today: Today, wind energy is an important source of renewable energy. Wind farms are being built around the world in coastal regions, in open fields and at sea. The technology for harnessing wind energy has improved significantly, and wind turbines are capable of generating large amounts of clean electricity.

The use of wind energy has evolved from the simple windmills of ancient times to state-of-the-art wind turbines that make a significant contribution to global energy supplies. It is an important pillar in the effort to reduce CO_2 emissions and switch to renewable energy sources.

1.2 Development of modern wind power technology

The development of modern wind power technology has a long history, dating back to the 19th century. Here is a summary of the key milestones:

Early Windmills (circa 1st century): The use of wind energy began with windmills, used primarily for grain grinding and water pumping. However, these windmills were not designed to generate electricity.

Wind Turbines in the 19th Century: In the 19th century, engineers began developing wind turbines that could be used to generate electricity. The Scot James Blyth is often cited as one of the first to build a wind turbine to generate electricity in 1887.

Large wind turbines in the 1940s: During World War II, larger wind turbines were developed in the United States and Europe to provide electricity in remote areas. However, these systems were not yet very efficient.

Emergence of modern wind energy in the 1970s: Wind energy experienced a boom in the 1970s. Rising oil prices, environmental awareness and advances in technology contributed to this. The first commercially successful wind farms were built in Denmark.

Introduction of variable speed wind turbines with power electronics: In the 1980s, variable speed turbines with power electronics were developed to increase efficiency and reduce load on turbines.

Offshore wind turbines: In the 1990s, the first offshore wind turbines were installed to make better use of the wind near the coast. These systems are generally larger and more efficient than onshore systems.

Technological Advances: Over the past few decades, wind power technology has made significant advances. This includes the development of larger and more powerful turbines, improved blade technology, more efficient generators and advanced control systems.

Integration of renewable energies: Wind energy plays an important role in the energy transition and is increasingly being integrated into the power grid. Combining wind energy with other renewable energy sources and energy storage technologies is being explored to ensure electricity supply reliability.

Future Prospects: Wind power technology continues to improve to reduce costs and increase efficiency. New developments in materials technology, smart grids and energy storage are expected to further strengthen the role of wind energy in global energy supplies.

The development of modern wind power technology has helped produce significant amounts of clean energy and contributed to reducing greenhouse gas emissions. It is playing an increasingly important role in the global energy transition towards more sustainable energy sources.

1.3 Milestones in the history of wind power

The history of wind power goes back a long way and has seen many milestones over time. Here are some important events and developments in wind power history:

Ancient Windmills: The use of windmills to generate energy and grind grain dates back to ancient times. Already in the 1st century BC. Windmills were used in Persia in the 1st century BC.

Dutch Windmills: In the 17th century, windmills reached their peak in the Netherlands and were used to irrigate agricultural land and generate energy for other purposes.

Electric wind generators: The Scot James Blyth built the first known wind generator to generate electricity in 1887. However, this was still quite small and had limited capacity.

Wind Generators in the 20th Century: Wind generators continued to be developed throughout the 20th century, particularly in the United States and Europe. However, these windmills were mostly small and were used for decentralized applications.

Oil crisis in the 1970s: Rising oil prices and increasing environmental pollution from fossil fuels led to increased interest in renewable energies, including wind energy.

Larger wind turbines: Starting in the 1980s, larger wind turbines were developed that could generate more energy. An important milestone was the introduction of variable speed wind turbines with rotor blades.

Offshore wind energy: The development of offshore wind farms, in which wind turbines are installed in the sea, began in the 1990s. This opened up new possibilities for the use of wind energy.

Technological Advances: Advances in aerodynamics, materials science and control engineering have resulted in more efficient and powerful wind turbines.

Renewable energy policy: The introduction of policy measures to promote renewable energy, such as feed-in tariffs and subsidies, contributed to the rapid spread of wind turbines.

Record performance and scale: In recent years, ever larger wind turbines have been developed that can generate significant amounts of clean electricity. Some offshore wind farms have reached impressive capacity.

These milestones show how wind power has evolved from a traditional use in windmills to one of today's most important renewable energy sources. Wind turbine technology and capacity are expected to continue to grow as the world increases its focus on renewable energy to reduce greenhouse gas emissions and combat climate change.

Chapter 2: Basics of Wind Energy

2.1 Wind as a renewable energy source

Wind energy is an important renewable energy source that is used to generate electricity by harnessing the kinetic energy of the wind. Here is some important information about wind energy:

How it works: Wind turbines, also known as wind turbines, consist of large rotor blades that rotate in the wind. This rotational movement is converted into electrical energy via a generator. The amount of energy produced depends on the wind speed and the size of the wind turbine.

Advantages of wind energy:

Environmentally friendly: Wind energy produces no greenhouse gas emissions or air pollution, helping to combat climate change.

Unlimited Resource: Wind is a renewable energy source that never runs out.

Low operating costs: Once installed, the operating costs of wind turbines are comparatively low.

Local economic development: Wind farms can create jobs in rural areas and stimulate local economies.

Challenges of wind energy:

Variability: Wind is not constant and can be unpredictable, which can affect the stability of the power grid.

Landscape intervention: Wind turbines require a lot of land or sea space, which can lead to landscape changes.

Bird strikes: Some types of wind turbines can endanger birds if they are located in bird migration routes.

Types of Wind Turbines: There are different types of wind turbines including:

Onshore wind turbines: These are located on land and are the most commonly used type.

Offshore wind turbines: These are located in the sea and have the potential to generate more energy, but are more expensive to install.

Small wind turbines: These are designed for use in residential areas or small businesses.

Technological advances: The efficiency and performance of wind turbines have improved significantly in recent years, making wind energy more competitive.

Wind energy is being actively promoted in many countries to reduce dependence on fossil fuels and accelerate the transition to clean energy. Wind energy can play an important role in reducing the environmental impact of energy consumption and helping to achieve climate goals.

2.2 Wind physics and aerodynamics

Wind physics and aerodynamics are two closely related areas of physics that deal with the behavior of air currents and their interaction with solid bodies. Here is a brief explanation of both concepts:

Wind physics : Wind physics deals with the fundamental principles of air currents in the atmosphere. She studies how winds form, move and change. Some important concepts and phenomena in wind physics are:

Air pressure : Differences in air pressure are responsible for the formation of winds. Air flows from areas of higher pressure to areas of lower pressure.

Wind speed : The speed of the wind is measured and analyzed. It can vary significantly depending on geographical location and weather conditions.

Wind direction : The direction from which the wind blows is also of interest and is often measured using wind vanes or anemometers.

Turbulence : Turbulence in airflow can impact aircraft, buildings and other structures.

Weather phenomena : Wind physicists are also involved in the study of weather phenomena such as storms, tornadoes and hurricanes.

Aerodynamics : Aerodynamics is a branch of fluid mechanics and focuses on the interaction between solid bodies (e.g. airplanes, cars, buildings) and the surrounding air. Aerodynamics deals with:

Lift and Drag : Aerodynamics explains how airplanes generate lift to stay in the air and how air resistance affects their movement.

Airfoils : It analyzes the airfoils around various objects and how they affect drag and stability.

Flow separation : This phenomenon occurs when airflow separates from the surface of an object and can lead to instability.

Shape optimization : Aerodynamicists design and optimize shapes of vehicles and structures to minimize drag and maximize efficiency.

2.3 Wind measurement and analysis

Wind measurement and analysis are important aspects in various fields such as meteorology, renewable energy, aviation, environmental science and civil engineering. Here is an overview of wind measurement and analysis:

Wind measurement:

Wind measuring devices: There are several types of wind measuring devices, including anemometers, wind vanes and lidar systems. These instruments record wind speed and direction.

Wind masts: Wind measurement masts are often used in the wind energy industry to collect accurate data at different heights. This data is crucial for the location selection of wind turbines.

Weather Balloons: In meteorology, weather balloons are used to obtain wind data in the atmosphere at different altitudes. This is important for weather forecasts and storm warnings.

Wind analysis:

Compass Roses: Compass Roses are charts that represent the frequency and direction of the wind in a particular region. They help identify wind patterns and trends.

Statistical analysis: By collecting wind data over time, statistics can be created to determine average wind speeds, wind directions, wind peaks and fluctuations.

Wind energy analysis: In the wind energy industry, wind analysis is carried out to predict the energy yield of wind turbines. This helps in planning wind farms and maximizing energy production.

Wind load analyses: In the construction industry, wind load analyzes are carried out to evaluate the effects of wind forces on buildings and structures. This is crucial for the safety and stability of structures.

Computer simulations: Complex wind flows can be analyzed with the help of computer models. These models are used, for example, in architecture to optimize the ventilation of buildings.

Environmental Impacts: Analyzing wind is also important for understanding environmental impacts such as air pollution, spread of pollutants, and spread of wildfires.

Wind measurement and analysis are therefore versatile tools used in various industries and scientific disciplines to obtain accurate information about the wind and understand its effects. This knowledge is crucial for planning, safety and efficiency in various application areas.

Chapter 3: Types of Wind Turbines

3.1 Horizontal vs. vertical axis wind turbines

Horizontal and vertical wind turbines are two different types of wind turbines used to generate electricity from wind energy. Each of these wind turbines has its own advantages and disadvantages:

Horizontal wind turbines (HAWT - Horizontal Axis Wind Turbines):

Efficiency: HAWTs are generally more efficient than vertical wind turbines. They make optimal use of the wind by automatically aligning themselves with the wind direction to achieve the maximum energy yield.

Greater power: HAWTs are capable of generating greater power and are therefore widely used in commercial wind farms.

Proven Technology: HAWTs are long established and well researched, resulting in mature technology and greater availability of spare parts.

Higher tower heights: Due to their design, HAWTs can easily be placed on taller towers to access higher wind speeds.

Vertical wind turbines (VAWT - Vertical Axis Wind Turbines):

Lower Visibility: VAWTs often have lower visibility and therefore may be less noticeable in urban areas.

Easier Maintenance: Because of their vertical orientation, VAWTs are often easier to access and may require less extensive maintenance.

More consistent energy production: VAWTs typically produce a more consistent energy output because they are less sensitive to changes in wind direction.

Lower overall height: They are typically shorter than HAWTs and therefore require shorter towers, which can be an advantage in certain environments.

It is important to note that the choice between horizontal and vertical wind turbines depends on various factors, including location, available wind resources, aesthetic concerns, installation costs, and intended application. Both types of wind turbines have their place in the wind energy industry, and choosing between them depends on the specific needs of a project.

3.2 Onshore vs. offshore wind turbines

Onshore and offshore wind turbines are two different types of wind turbines used to generate electricity from wind energy. They differ mainly in their location and characteristics. Here are the key differences between onshore and offshore wind turbines:

Location:

Onshore wind turbines are located on land, usually on hills, near the coast or in flat areas with sufficient wind potential.

Offshore wind turbines are installed in the sea or in large inland bodies of water, often near the coast, but also further away from the coast in the open sea.

Installation:

Onshore wind turbines are generally easier to install and require less complex construction projects compared to offshore turbines.

Offshore wind turbines require significantly more technical challenges and investments due to the more difficult site accessibility and installation at sea.

Wind conditions:

Offshore wind turbines benefit from more consistent and stronger winds compared to onshore turbines. This leads to higher utilization and productivity.

Onshore wind turbines can be influenced by local topographic features and vegetation that make wind patterns more variable.

Environmental impact:

Onshore wind turbines typically have lower environmental impacts and are easier to manage in terms of environmental protection and permitting procedures.

Offshore wind turbines can potentially have greater impacts on marine ecosystems and wildlife, but also require strict environmental regulations and protection measures.

Cost:

Onshore wind turbines are generally cheaper to build and maintain.

Offshore wind turbines are more expensive to install and maintain, but the higher energy production may justify the cost in the long term.

Energy yield:

Offshore wind turbines tend to have higher capacity and generate more electricity per turbine compared to onshore turbines.

Visibility and acceptance:

Onshore wind turbines are often more visible and may be less acceptable due to aesthetic concerns.

Offshore wind turbines are often less visible to the public, which can make them easier to accept.

The choice between onshore and offshore wind turbines depends on various factors, including the availability of suitable sites, costs, environmental impacts and regulatory requirements. In many cases, a combination of both technologies is used to take advantage of both approaches and maximize wind energy production.

3.3 Small vs. large wind turbines

Small and large wind turbines differ in many ways, from their size and performance to the applications for which they are best suited. Here are some key differences between small and large wind turbines:

Size and performance:

Small wind turbines typically have a power rating of less than 100 kilowatts (kW), while large wind turbines can have power ratings of several megawatts (MW). The exact boundary between small and large facilities can vary depending on the region and definition.

Height and rotor blades:

Large wind turbines are significantly higher than small turbines. The tower height of large systems can easily reach 100 meters or more, while small systems usually have shorter towers.

The blades of large turbines are also much longer and have a larger diameter, allowing them to capture more wind and therefore produce more energy.

Locations:

Small wind turbines are often designed for decentralized applications in rural areas or on private properties. For example, they can be used to supply individual houses or farms.

Large wind turbines are usually installed in wind farms at locations with high wind speeds. They are often built in coastal areas or on windy plateaus.

Costs and maintenance:

Small wind turbines are generally cheaper to purchase and require less maintenance than large systems.

Large wind turbines have higher initial costs and require careful maintenance and servicing to ensure maximum efficiency and service life.

Power grid integration:

Large wind turbines are more suitable for integration into the power grid and can generate a significant amount of electrical energy that is fed into the public grid.

Small wind turbines are often used for off-grid applications and are less focused on grid integration.

Environmental impact:

Large wind turbines have potentially greater environmental impacts, particularly in terms of landscape, bird and bat strikes and noise pollution, than small turbines. However, this depends on various factors including the location and type of facility.

The choice between small and large wind turbines depends on various factors, including available land, local wind resources, financial resources and intended use. Both types of wind turbines play an important role in harnessing renewable energy and reducing dependence on fossil fuels.

Chapter 4: Structure and functionality of wind turbines

4.1 The main components of a wind turbine

A wind turbine is made up of several main components that work together to convert wind energy into electrical energy. Here are the key components of a typical wind turbine:

Rotor blades: The rotor blades are the part of the wind turbine that captures the wind. They are usually designed in the form of large blades and are attached to the hub of the wind turbine.

Hub: The hub is the central component of the wind turbine to which the rotor blades are attached. The hub rotates with the rotor blades and transmits the rotational movement to the shaft.

Rotor Shaft: The rotor shaft is a long, rigid shaft connected to the hub. The rotational movement of the rotor blades is transmitted to the rotor shaft.

Gearbox: Many wind turbines have a gearbox that increases the speed of rotation of the rotor shaft to bring the generator shaft to the higher speed required to produce electricity.

Generator: The generator is the heart of the wind turbine. It converts the mechanical energy of the rotating rotor shaft into electrical energy. This occurs by inducing electricity in copper coils within the generator.

Nacelle: The nacelle is the housing that contains the generator and other electrical components. It is usually placed at the top of the wind turbine tower and can rotate with the blades to direct the wind.

Tower: The tower is the structure that raises the nacelle and stabilizes the entire wind turbine. Towers can be built at different heights to take advantage of higher wind speeds at higher altitudes.

Control system: A control system monitors and controls the various components of the wind turbine to ensure that they operate efficiently and safely. This includes pointing the blades into the wind, monitoring wind speed and optimizing performance.

Transformer: The transformer increases the voltage of the electricity generated in order to be able to feed it into the power grid.

Foundation: The foundation is the base on which the wind turbine tower stands. It must be strong enough to support the weight of the system and protect it from wind and weather.

These major components work together to convert wind energy into electrical energy and feed it into the electrical grid to power homes and businesses.

4.2 Wind rotor and blade shape

Wind rotors are the rotating components of a wind turbine that convert the kinetic energy of the wind into mechanical energy. The shape of the blades and the design of the wind rotors are crucial for the efficiency and performance of a wind turbine. Here are some important aspects of wind rotor blade shape:

Profile shape: The blades of a wind rotor often have an aerodynamic profile shape similar to that of aircraft wings. This shape helps optimize airflow and create the lift that propels the blades.

Length and size: The length of the wind rotor blades varies depending on the type of system and location. Larger blades can capture more wind and therefore generate more energy. However, they are also heavier and require more stable structures.

Materials: Most wind rotor blades are made of glass fiber reinforced plastic or carbon fiber composite materials. These materials are lightweight yet strong enough to withstand the stresses encountered during operation.

Profile adjustment: Modern wind turbines often have variable profile adjustment blades that can automatically adjust to wind conditions. This allows for optimal performance in different wind speeds.

Number of Blades: Most wind turbines have either three or two blades on their rotors. The number of blades affects the efficiency and aerodynamic properties of the rotor.

The blade shape and design are carefully optimized by engineers and designers to ensure the best possible performance and energy production under the given conditions. This can also vary from location to location as wind conditions can vary.

It is important to note that technology in the field of wind turbines is constantly evolving, and there are many different designs and approaches to increasing efficiency and reducing costs.

4.3 Generators and turbines

Wind turbine : The wind turbine is the part of the wind turbine that converts the kinetic energy of the wind into mechanical energy. It consists of several main components:

Rotor Blades : The rotor blades are aerodynamically shaped blades that rotate around a horizontal shaft. They capture the wind and convert it into rotational energy.

Hub : The hub is the central part of the wind turbine to which the rotor blades are attached. The kinetic energy generated by the rotor blades is transferred to the hub.

Gearbox : In some wind turbines, a gearbox is used to convert the low rotational speed of the blades into a higher speed more suitable for the generator.

Generator : The generator is the heart of the wind turbine. It converts the mechanical energy generated by the wind turbine into electrical energy. There are different types of generators used in wind turbines including:

Asynchronous or induction generator : This type is often used in older wind turbines. It generates alternating current (AC) and does not require an external power supply to start.

Synchronous generator : Synchronous generators also produce alternating current and are widely used in modern wind turbines. However, they require an external power supply to start up and be synchronized to the correct frequency.

Permanent Magnet Synchronous Generator (PMG) : PMG generators are more efficient than other types and do not require external power to start. They can be found in many modern wind turbines.

The generator is connected to the hub of the wind turbine, and as the blades rotate, the mechanical energy is transferred to the generator. The generator converts this energy into electrical power, which can then be fed through the network or stored in batteries.

The efficient conversion of wind energy into electrical energy requires complex control and regulation systems to ensure that the wind turbine always responds optimally to the wind conditions and achieves the maximum energy yield.

4.4 Control and monitoring systems

The control and monitoring systems of a wind turbine are crucial for its safe and efficient operation. These systems ensure that the system functions properly, adapts to environmental conditions and reacts quickly in the event of problems. Here are some of the main components and functions of a typical wind turbine control and monitoring system:

Wind measurement: The system is equipped with wind measuring devices to record the wind speed and direction in real time. This data is used to set the optimal angle of the rotor blades and adapt the operation of the turbine to the current wind conditions.

Performance optimization: The system constantly analyzes the wind turbine's performance and adjusts the settings to achieve the maximum energy output in the prevailing wind conditions. This may include adjusting blade angles and generator speed.

Monitoring of mechanical components: Sensors monitor the condition of the rotor blades, gearbox, bearings and other mechanical components. Irregularities or signs of wear are detected and reported to enable preventative maintenance.

Safety systems: The facility is equipped with safety systems that can stop operations in the event of strong winds or other dangerous situations to prevent damage. This can include braking the rotor blades or turning off the generator.

Data transmission and remote monitoring: The collected data is transmitted in real time to a central control center. This allows technicians to continuously monitor and diagnose problems, even remotely.

Maintenance planning: The system creates maintenance plans based on the operating data and wear of the system. This makes maintenance more efficient and cost-optimized.

Grid integration: The wind turbine is integrated into the power grid and communicates with the grid to ensure that the energy generated is fed in and distributed efficiently.

Data collection and analysis: Collected data is used for long-term analysis and improvement of equipment efficiency. This can help increase yield and extend the life of the plant.

Communication systems: The turbine can also communicate with other wind turbines in the area to enable performance coordination and optimization in a wind farm.

The control and monitoring systems of a wind turbine are extremely complex and play a central role in generating wind energy in a safe, efficient and environmentally friendly manner. They allow the system to be controlled and monitored in real time to ensure optimal performance and reliability.

Chapter 5: Site selection and planning of wind farms

5.1 Selection of the appropriate location

Selecting the appropriate location for a wind farm is a crucial step in developing a successful wind energy project. Here are some important steps and factors to consider when choosing a suitable location for a wind farm:

Wind resource analysis:

Measuring and analyzing wind speeds at potential locations is critical. It is important to use long-term wind data to accurately assess wind resources.

Availability of Land:

The availability of sufficient land is crucial for building a wind farm. The size of land required depends on the number and size of wind turbines.

Environmental impact:

A comprehensive environmental impact assessment (EIA) should be carried out to ensure that the wind farm will not have a negative impact on wildlife, the landscape or other environmental aspects.

Mains connection:

Proximity to existing power grids or the ability to connect to the grid is important in order to feed the energy generated into the power grid.

Approvals and regulations:

Compliance with all local, regional and national regulations and permits is essential. This often includes noise regulations, building regulations and environmental laws.

Topography and terrain:

The topography of the site can influence wind flow. Locations with uninterrupted and good wind flow are preferred.

Economic considerations:

The economic viability of the project is crucial. This includes analyzing capital costs, operating and maintenance costs, as well as calculating the expected return and payback period.

Acceptance in the community:

The acceptance and support of the local community is important. Communication and community participation can avoid conflict.

Technical infrastructure:

The availability of roads, bridges and other infrastructure facilities can significantly influence the construction and maintenance of the wind farm.

Risk assessment:

A comprehensive risk assessment should be carried out to identify possible obstacles and risks and develop strategies to deal with them.

Selecting the site for a wind farm requires careful planning and analysis to ensure the project is successful and sustainable.

5.2 Environmental impacts and approval procedures

Developing a wind farm is a complex process that must take into account various environmental impacts and go through numerous approvals. Here are some of the important steps and considerations associated with the environmental impact and permitting process for a wind farm:

1. **Site selection:** Site selection is crucial. Various factors must be considered, including wind resources, terrain conditions, proximity to power grid infrastructure and potential environmental impacts.

2. **Environmental impact studies:** Before a wind farm can be approved, comprehensive environmental impact studies must

be carried out. These studies examine potential impacts on wildlife, landscape, noise and other environmental aspects.

3. Approval procedures: Approval procedures vary depending on the country and region. They may require federal, state and local permits. For example, in the United States, permits may be required from the Federal Aviation Administration (FAA), state and local authorities.

4. Public Participation: In many cases, developers are required to conduct public hearings and consultations to gather the opinions of residents and stakeholders and address potential concerns.

5. Nature conservation and habitat preservation: The protection of wild animals and their habitats is an important aspect in the development of wind farms. Measures can be taken to protect birds and bats from collisions with the wind turbines.

6. Noise protection: Wind turbines produce noise that can disturb residents. Therefore, noise control measures must be taken to ensure that noise limits are met.

7. Landscape preservation: The design of the wind farm should impact the landscape as little as possible. This can be achieved by selecting appropriate locations and turbine designs.

8. Sustainability and resource consumption: The manufacture, installation and maintenance of wind turbines requires resources. Considering environmental impacts throughout the turbines' life cycle is important.

9. Operating permits: After installation, operating permits must be obtained to ensure that the wind farm is properly maintained and operated.

10. Monitoring and Compliance: Developers are often required to monitor environmental impacts during operations and ensure they comply with applicable environmental regulations.

5.3 Layout and design of wind farms

The layout and design of wind farms are crucial aspects in the planning and construction of wind turbines. A well-thought-out layout and design can significantly impact the efficiency and profitability of a wind farm. Here are some important factors and considerations related to wind farm layout and design:

Location selection:

Choosing the right location is the first step. Locations with high and consistent wind speeds are crucial to maximize energy production.

Environmental impacts, nature reserves and local communities also need to be taken into account.

Wind turbine placement:

The placement of the wind turbines in the wind farm is of great importance. The turbines should be arranged so that they do not shade each other in the wind (wake effect), as this reduces energy production.

The turbines should be arranged in a regular pattern or rows to make efficient use of space.

Turbine type and size:

Choosing the right type and size of turbine depends on the specific wind conditions at the site. Larger turbines can produce more energy, but also require more space and infrastructure.

Infrastructure and access:

Planning roads, cable routes and foundations for the turbines is important to ensure efficient installation and maintenance of the systems.

Access to the wind farm for maintenance and repair work must be taken into account.

Environmental Impacts and Permits:

Environmental impacts on birds, bats and other animals need to be analyzed. This may result in certain areas of the wind farm being closed or certain measures being taken to minimize these impacts.

Permits from state and local authorities are required and planning must comply with applicable regulations and laws.

Mains connection:

The connection of the wind farm to the power grid is crucial. The infrastructure for electricity transmission must be planned and built.

Landscaping and integration:

The design of the wind farm should fit into the surrounding area and impact the landscape as little as possible.

In some cases, the integration of wind turbines into agricultural land or forest areas may be considered to continue agricultural production or forestry.

Security:

The safety of workers and the public must be guaranteed. This requires clear security policies and procedures.

Operation and maintenance planning:

An effective operations and maintenance plan is crucial to ensure the long-term performance of wind turbines.

Chapter 6: Wind energy and the environment

6.1 Environmental benefits of wind turbines

Wind turbines offer a number of environmental benefits that make them a sustainable energy source. Here are some of the key environmental benefits of wind turbines:

Reducing greenhouse gas emissions: Wind turbines generate electricity without direct emissions of greenhouse gases such as carbon dioxide (CO_2). This helps reduce global warming and climate change.

Air quality: Unlike fossil-fuelled power plants, wind turbines do not emit air pollutants such as sulfur dioxide or nitrogen oxides, which contribute to air pollution and health problems.

Water Consumption: Compared to conventional power plants, which require large amounts of water to generate electricity, wind turbines typically do not require water except for occasional maintenance and cleaning.

Land use: Wind turbines take up relatively little land, allowing the land beneath them to continue to be used for agricultural purposes or nature reserves.

Avoidance of resource extraction: Although the manufacture of wind turbines requires certain materials such as steel and concrete, they avoid the continuous need for fossil fuels associated with mining and the extraction of coal, oil and gas.

Noise emissions: Modern wind turbines are generally quiet and have little impact on the surrounding area. This can be viewed as positive in comparison to other industrial facilities or transport routes.

Energy independence: Wind power can help reduce dependence on fossil fuels and imports as it is a domestic, renewable energy source.

Biodiversity: Wind turbines near wind farms can help maintain habitats for certain animal species, as the areas beneath the turbines often remain undisturbed and accessible to wildlife.

However, it is important to note that wind turbines can also have certain environmental impacts, particularly in relation to bird and bat mortality and landscape aesthetics. Therefore, careful site selection and environmental assessment is crucial to minimize negative impacts and maximize the benefits of wind energy .

6.2 Environmental impacts and their minimization

Wind turbines have some environmental impacts that must be taken into account when designing, installing and operating them. Here are some of the main environmental impacts of wind turbines and ways to minimize them:

Bird strike : Birds can collide with the rotating blades of wind turbines. To minimize this problem, bird migration and bird behavior studies are conducted to choose locations with low bird migration. Radar and camera systems can also be used to detect birds and switch off the systems if necessary.

Bat protection : Bats are also at risk of colliding with the rotor blades. Ultra-clear acoustic devices and thermal cameras can be used to detect bats and turn off the systems when they are nearby.

Noise pollution : Wind turbines produce noise that can disturb residents. By choosing locations that are sufficiently away from residential areas and using modern, quiet turbines, noise pollution can be minimized.

Landscape and aesthetics : Wind turbines can change the landscape and be perceived as disturbing. Careful site selection, consideration of community input, and design of landscape improvements near facilities can help minimize aesthetic impacts.

Ground changes : The construction work for wind turbines requires ground interventions. To minimize impacts on the soil, reforestation and restoration measures should be carried out to restore the soil to its original state.

Disturbance to wildlife : The construction of wind turbines can disrupt wildlife habitats. By limiting land use, planting native plants and establishing conservation zones, these impacts can be minimized.

Resource Consumption : Manufacturing wind turbines requires materials and energy. One way to minimize resource consumption is to use more efficient production methods and rely on recycling and reusing materials.

Energy storage : Because wind energy is not constant, storing excess energy for periods of low wind is important. The development of efficient energy storage technologies such as batteries can help increase the reliability of wind turbines.

Minimizing the environmental impact of wind turbines requires comprehensive planning, site selection and technology development. Through continuous research and development, wind turbines can be made even more environmentally friendly in the future. It is important that environmental impacts are considered throughout the entire life cycle of wind turbines to ensure sustainable use of renewable energy sources.

6.3 Bird protection and wind energy

Bird protection in connection with wind turbines (WEA) is an important aspect in the planning, construction and operation of wind turbines. Wind turbines can have an impact on birds, particularly migratory birds and birds of prey. Here are some key aspects of bird conservation related to wind turbines:

Site selection: The site selection for wind turbines should be done carefully to avoid areas with high bird populations. This often requires extensive study and research to understand the flight patterns of birds in the region.

Bird monitoring: Monitoring of bird populations is necessary before and after the installation of wind turbines in order to detect changes in the populations. This can be done through visual observations, radar technology and other methods.

Collision risk: One of the main dangers for birds near wind turbines is collision with the rotor blades. In order to minimize the risk of collision, measures such as switching off systems during bird migration or slowing down the rotor blades during periods of low wind are often taken.

Habitat loss: The construction of wind turbines can alter or destroy habitat for birds. This can be minimized through careful site selection and habitat restoration near facilities.

Species protection: In some cases, particularly endangered bird species may be endangered by the construction of wind turbines. In such cases, special protective measures are required to ensure that the facilities do not have a negative impact on these species.

Research and technology: The development of technologies such as radar and camera systems for bird detection as well as research into bird behavior patterns near wind turbines are helping to find better solutions for bird protection.

It is important to emphasize that bird protection and wind energy development do not necessarily have to be in conflict. With careful planning, technological innovations and compliance with regulations, wind turbines can be operated in an environmentally friendly manner while minimizing the impact on birds. However, this requires close collaboration between environmental organizations, the wind energy industry and governments to develop and enforce best practices and policies.

Chapter 7: Economics of Wind Power Projects

7.1 Costs and Financing

The cost and financing of wind turbines can vary significantly depending on location, size, technology and other factors. Here are some important aspects about the cost and financing of wind turbines:

System costs: The costs of building a wind turbine depend on the size and type of the system. Larger systems are generally more expensive. Costs may also vary from location to location as accessibility and wind conditions must be taken into account.

Operating costs: In addition to the system costs, there are also ongoing costs during operation. This includes maintenance, repairs, insurance and, if necessary, rent for the land on which the system is located.

Financing: Financing wind turbines can be done in different ways. Here are some options:

Equity: A company or investor can finance the investment with its own capital, either alone or in partnership with other investors.

Debt capital: Many wind power projects are financed through loans or bonds. Banks and financial institutions are often willing to provide loans for renewable energy.

Funding: In some countries there are state or regional funding programs that offer financial incentives for the construction of wind turbines, such as feed-in tariffs or investment subsidies.

Equity financing: It is also possible for several investors to jointly participate in a wind power project and share the costs.

Return expectations: Investors expect a return on their invested capital. The return depends on the expected income from the sale of the electricity generated as well as the operating and financing costs.

Sales of energy: The sale of the electricity generated is an important source of income for wind turbine operators. This can be done through long-term power purchase agreements (PPAs) with utility companies or direct sales to the electricity market.

Risks: Investments in wind turbines involve various risks, including technical failures, fluctuations in wind speeds, regulatory changes and market risks. A careful risk assessment is crucial.

Payback and profit: The payback period (time required to recover the initial investment) and the expected profit depend on the costs, revenues and operating costs. Typically, investors seek to shorten the payback period and ensure long-term profitable operations.

Environmental Impact: Wind turbines are an environmentally friendly source of energy and can help reduce greenhouse gas emissions and reduce environmental impact. This may provide additional incentives and support for the construction of wind turbines in some regions.

Overall, the costs and financing of wind turbines are complex and depend on many factors. In most cases, the profitability of wind power projects can be attractive in the long term, especially if the systems are well maintained and energy prices remain stable or increase.

7.2 Return on Investment (ROI)

The return on investment (ROI) of wind turbines depends on various factors and can vary depending on the location, size of the system, investment costs and electricity generation. ROI is a metric that shows how profitable an investment is in relation to the expenses incurred.

Here are some important factors that can affect wind turbine ROI:

Location : Location is crucial. Wind turbines produce more electricity in places with stronger and more consistent winds. A well-chosen location can significantly increase profitability.

System Type : There are different types of wind turbines, from small home-use wind turbines to large multi-turbine wind farms. Choosing the right type of system has a direct impact on the investment costs and the amount of energy generated.

Investment costs : The purchase and installation of a wind turbine requires considerable investment. The ROI depends heavily on the total costs.

Electricity generation : The amount of electricity generated depends on the size of the system, wind conditions and system availability. Higher electricity production leads to higher revenue.

Operating and maintenance costs : The ongoing operating and maintenance costs influence the profitability of the system. Efficiently managing these costs can improve ROI.

Electricity prices : The level of compensation or sales price for the electricity generated can vary greatly and influences revenue and ROI.

Subsidies and Incentives : Governments and local authorities often offer subsidies and incentives for renewable energy, which can positively impact ROI.

System lifespan : The lifespan of the wind turbine influences the length of time in which ROI is achieved. Typically, wind turbines have a lifespan of 20 to 25 years or more.

To calculate the ROI for a specific wind turbine, you would need to consider the investment costs, expected revenue from electricity sales, operation and maintenance costs, and other relevant factors. The exact calculation can be complex and often requires extensive economic analysis. A positive ROI indicates that the investment is profitable and generating profits. An ROI below 100% means that the investment did not cover the entire cost.

It is also important to note that the profitability of wind turbines can increase over time as the investment costs are depreciated and the income from electricity sales continues to flow.

7.3 Subsidies and Incentives

Wind turbine subsidies and incentives are measures taken by governments and other institutions to promote the development and use of wind energy. These measures are intended to help increase the use of renewable energy, combat climate change and reduce dependence on fossil fuels. Here are some examples of wind turbine subsidies and incentives:

Feed-in tariffs: Governments can introduce feed-in tariffs under which wind turbine operators receive a fixed compensation per kilowatt hour of electricity produced. These tariffs guarantee investors a certain return and promote the profitability of wind power projects.

Investment grants: Governments or regional authorities often provide direct financial support in the form of grants for the construction of wind turbines. These grants can significantly reduce initial investment costs.

Tax Benefits: Tax benefits, such as tax breaks, depreciation and tax credits, can provide financial incentives to wind turbine investors and operators.

Grid access and priority: Preferential injection of wind energy into the grid can encourage operators to invest in wind turbines as it ensures that the electricity generated is prioritized.

Renewable energy support programs: Governments can set up special support programs aimed at the development of renewable energy. These programs often provide financial incentives and technical assistance for wind power projects.

Renewable energy certificates: Issuing renewable energy certificates can help increase the value of wind energy by allowing operators to generate additional revenue from the sale of such certificates.

Research and development funding: Governments and institutions can promote wind energy research and development to support technological advances and cost reductions.

Environmental regulations and emissions reduction: Certain countries or regions may set environmental regulations and emissions targets that require the expansion of renewable energy such as wind power. Operators can be financially rewarded if they help reduce greenhouse gas emissions.

These subsidies and incentives may vary by country, region and political climate. Its main objective is to reduce the cost of installing wind turbines, increase profitability and promote the use of clean energy to reduce environmental impact and accelerate the transition to more sustainable energy sources.

Chapter 8: Technological Trends and Innovations

8.1 Advances in wind power technology

Advances in wind power technology are critical to making renewable energy sources more efficient and competitive. Here are some of the key developments and advances in wind power technology:

Larger turbines : One of the most noticeable developments is the increase in the size of wind turbines. Larger blades and towers make it possible to capture more wind and therefore generate more energy.

Higher towers : Wind turbines are being placed on ever higher towers to take advantage of higher wind speeds at greater altitudes. This increases the energy yield and enables use in regions with lower wind speeds.

More efficient rotor blades : Advances in aerodynamics and materials science have resulted in rotor blades being lighter while also being more resistant to wind loads.

Intelligent control systems : State-of-the-art wind turbine control technologies optimize performance in real time. This involves adjusting blade angles and speed to maximize energy output while minimizing load on the turbine.

Repair and maintenance : Improvements in condition monitoring and drone technology enable early detection of problems and more efficient maintenance of wind turbines.

Floating wind farms : The development of floating wind farms opens up new opportunities for wind energy utilization in deep water where solid foundations are not feasible.

Wind energy storage : Combining wind turbines with advanced energy storage technologies, such as batteries, enables continuous power supply even when the wind is not blowing.

Networked wind farms : Intelligent networking of wind farms enables better integration of wind energy into the power grid and increased efficiency.

Material innovations : New materials such as carbon fiber are being used in turbine manufacturing to reduce weight and improve performance.

Recycling and sustainability : The industry is working on solutions for the environmentally friendly disposal of wind turbines that are no longer used to improve sustainability.

These advances in wind power technology have helped make wind energy one of the most cost-effective and fastest-growing energy sources in the world. They also help drive the transition to clean energy and reduce carbon emissions.

8.2 Storage technologies and network integration

Storage technologies and grid integration play a crucial role in modern energy supply and are essential components for integrating renewable energy sources, increasing efficiency and ensuring a stable power supply. Here are some important aspects and technologies related to storage technologies and their integration into energy networks:

Battery storage : Battery storage is one of the most common forms of energy storage. They store electrical energy in chemical form and can release it later. Lithium-ion batteries are particularly common, but there are also other technologies such as lead-acid batteries, redox flow batteries, and more.

Pumped storage power plants : Pumped storage power plants are a proven technology for storing energy. They use water reservoirs at different altitudes and can pump water up when necessary and then run it back down through turbines to generate electricity.

Thermal storage systems : These systems store energy in the form of heat. Examples include concentrating solar power plants with heat storage and latent heat storage, which store energy through changes in the physical state of a material.

Grid integration : The integration of energy storage into the power grid is crucial to ensure the stability and reliability of the grid. This requires advanced control systems and intelligent grid technologies.

Decentralized storage : Small decentralized storage systems such as home batteries are becoming increasingly important as they can increase self-consumption of solar energy and help reduce the load on the power grid.

Grid services : Energy storage can provide grid services such as frequency regulation, peak load shaving and grid support. These services are crucial to ensure network stability.

Energy storage in the transport sector : Batteries are also increasingly being used in electric vehicles, which opens up the possibility of using them as mobile energy storage devices and integrating them into the power grid.

Hydrogen as a storage medium : Hydrogen can serve as an energy storage medium by converting excess energy into the form of hydrogen gas and later used in fuel cells to generate electricity.

Long-term storage : Technologies such as underground compressed air storage and geothermal storage are under development for long-term storage of renewable energy.

Regulatory framework : The integration of storage technologies often requires an adjustment of the regulatory framework to create incentives for investments and operations.

Overall, storage technologies and grid integration play a central role in the transformation of the energy system towards renewable energy sources and a more sustainable energy supply. They make it possible to store excess energy so that it can then be made available when needed, thereby helping to stabilize the power grid.

8.3 Future prospects and challenges

Future prospects and challenges are important aspects in almost every area, be it in economy, technology, the environment or society. Below I will outline some general future prospects and challenges:

1. Technological Advancements:

Technology will continue to advance rapidly, particularly in areas such as artificial intelligence, robotics, quantum computing and biotechnology. These developments can have significant impacts on the economy, work and society.

2. Digitalization:

Digitalization will advance in almost all sectors, bringing with it both opportunities and risks. The interconnection of devices (Internet of Things) and the development of 5G and later 6G networks will continue to change the way we work and live.

3. Environment and sustainability:

Climate change and resource scarcity will continue to pose serious challenges. Finding sustainable solutions for energy production, agriculture, transportation and other areas will be crucial.

4. Health and Medicine:

Advances in medical research could lead to revolutionary treatments and cures. At the same time, healthcare systems worldwide are faced with the challenge of coping with rising costs and an aging population.

5. Demographic changes:

The population structures in many countries are changing, with the proportion of older people increasing. This presents societies with issues of pension provision and health care.

6. Globalization and geopolitical tensions:

Globalization continues, but it also faces challenges such as trade disputes and geopolitical tensions that can impact international cooperation.

7. Education and lifelong learning:

Education and skills requirements are changing rapidly, and lifelong learning is becoming increasingly important to achieve professional success.

8. Data protection and ethics:

As data collection and use increases, privacy issues and ethical concerns become more pressing. Protecting personal data and preventing misuse are key challenges.

9. Infrastructure and Sustainability:

The modernization and sustainability of infrastructure, including transport systems and urban development, will be a priority in many countries.

10. Social Changes:

Societies will continue to change, influenced by social trends such as urbanization, migration, social inequality and cultural diversity.

Addressing these future prospects and challenges requires close collaboration at global, national and local levels, innovative solutions and the adaptability of individuals and organizations. It will also be important to put long-term goals and sustainability at the heart of decision-making processes to create a better future for everyone.

Chapter 9: Global Wind Energy and Market Analysis

9.1 Worldwide distribution of wind turbines

The global adoption of wind turbines has increased significantly in recent years as many countries increasingly rely on renewable energy sources to meet their energy needs and combat climate change. Here is some important information about the global spread of wind turbines:

Regions with high wind energy production:

Europe: Countries such as Germany, Spain, Denmark and the Netherlands are leaders in wind energy production. Offshore wind farms in the North Sea are also important.

China: China is the world's largest producer of wind energy. The country has developed large wind power capacities both on land and offshore.

North America: The USA and Canada have significantly expanded their wind energy capacity in recent years, particularly in states such as Texas and Iowa.

Offshore wind energy: More and more countries are investing in offshore wind farms near the coast to create additional electricity generation capacity. Great Britain, Germany, the Netherlands and China are among the pioneers in this area.

Technological Advances: Advances in wind power technology have increased the efficiency of wind turbines and reduced costs. This has helped wind energy become more competitive in many countries.

Expansion goals and political support: Many countries have set ambitious goals for the expansion of wind energy in order to reduce their dependence on fossil fuels and achieve their climate goals. Political measures and subsidies support the expansion of wind energy.

Environmental Impacts and Challenges: Although wind energy is considered environmentally friendly, there are also challenges such as bird strikes, landscape changes and noise pollution to consider. The expansion of wind turbines requires careful site selection and environmental impact assessments.

The global adoption of wind turbines is expected to continue to increase as more countries switch to renewable energy to meet their energy needs and minimize the environmental impact of climate change. It is expected that technology will continue to improve and wind energy will make an important contribution to global energy supplies.

9.2 Market trends and developments

Wind turbine market trends and developments have changed significantly in recent years and are expected to continue to be dynamic in the future. Here are some of the key trends and developments in the wind turbine sector:

Technological Advances : The wind power industry has made significant progress in the development of wind turbine technologies. Larger blades, more efficient generators and advanced control systems have significantly improved the efficiency and performance of wind turbines.

Growth of offshore wind energy : Offshore wind farms built in the sea have become an important part of the wind energy mix. These systems benefit from constant winds and can be built in larger quantities. This is leading to increasing globalization of the wind energy industry.

Competitive costs : The cost of installing wind turbines has fallen in recent years, making wind energy one of the most competitive sources of energy. This trend is expected to continue as technology becomes more efficient and economies of scale increase.

Integrated energy systems : The integration of wind energy into the power grid is becoming increasingly important. Advances in energy storage and smart grid technologies are enabling more robust integration of wind turbines into the energy system.

Repowering and retrofitting : Older wind turbines are often replaced or upgraded with more modern and more powerful models in order to extend the life and performance of the turbines.

Market growth in emerging markets : Emerging countries are investing more in renewable energies, including wind power. This leads to significant growth in the market outside developed countries.

Sustainability requirements : Consumers, investors and governments are increasingly focusing on sustainability and environmental compatibility. This is leading to increased pressure on the wind power industry to promote environmentally friendly practices and technologies.

Policy support and regulation : Government support and regulation plays a crucial role in the development of the wind power industry. Long-term political commitments to support renewable energy are crucial.

Challenges in grid integration : The expansion of wind turbines can in some cases lead to challenges in grid integration because electricity generation is weather-dependent. However, the development of smart grid technologies and energy storage solutions will help address these challenges.

Innovation in turbine design : Research and development focuses on improving the efficiency and performance of wind turbines, including new designs such as vertical wind turbines and floating wind turbines.

These trends and developments suggest that the wind power industry will continue to play an important role in the global energy transition. The technology will become more efficient and cost-effective while contributing to a more sustainable energy supply.

9.3 International cooperation and agreements

International cooperation and agreements for wind turbines are crucial to promote the expansion of renewable energies worldwide and combat climate change. Here are some of the most important international initiatives and agreements in the field of wind energy:

International Agreement on Renewable Energy (IRENA) : The International Renewable Energy Agency (IRENA) is an international organization focused on the promotion and expansion of renewable energy, including wind energy. IRENA has member countries from around the world and promotes collaboration on technology development, policy making and capacity building.

European Union (EU) : The EU has ambitious targets for renewable energy, including wind power. The EU's renewable energy directive package requires member states to generate significant amounts of their electricity from renewable sources such as wind. There are also programs to promote cross-border electricity transmission in order to efficiently use generated wind power.

North Sea wind energy cooperation : States bordering the North Sea have come together to promote the development of offshore wind farms in the region. This includes the construction of wind turbines in international waters and the exchange of experiences and resources.

International wind energy agreements : There are various bilateral and multilateral agreements between countries that promote the development of wind energy. For example,

Germany and Denmark have close cooperation in wind energy development, particularly in the offshore sector.

Global wind energy associations : Organizations such as the Global Wind Energy Council (GWEC) work to represent the wind energy industry internationally and promote best practices. They organize events and promote the exchange of knowledge between countries and companies.

United Nations Climate Change Agreement (UNFCCC) : The Paris Agreement, concluded under the UN Framework Convention on Climate Change (UNFCCC), aims to limit global temperature rise. Wind energy is recognized as an important measure to reduce greenhouse gas emissions in this agreement.

International financing and support : International financial institutions such as the World Bank and the European Investment Bank provide financial support for wind energy projects in developing countries. This promotes the expansion of wind energy in regions with great potential.

These international collaborations and agreements are crucial to promoting wind energy worldwide and driving the transition to renewable energy. They allow countries to share knowledge, access finance and collaborate on the development of wind energy projects, ultimately helping to reduce greenhouse gas emissions and combat climate change.

Chapter 10: Wind power and the energy transition

10.1 Wind energy as a contribution to the energy transition

Wind energy plays a crucial role in implementing the energy transition, especially in countries that have set themselves the goal of increasingly meeting their energy needs from renewable sources. Here are some ways wind energy contributes to the energy transition:

Carbon dioxide reduction : Wind turbines generate electricity without direct CO2 emissions. This helps reduce greenhouse gas emissions, which is crucial to achieving climate goals and combating climate change.

Renewable Energy Source : Wind energy is a renewable energy source that never runs out. It is in contrast to fossil fuels, which are finite and lead to shortages and rising prices.

Diversification of energy supply : Wind energy contributes to the diversification of energy sources, which reduces dependence on fossil fuels and increases energy supply security.

Job creation : The wind energy industry creates jobs in the manufacturing, installation, maintenance and operation of wind turbines, which contributes to economic development.

Local Revenue : Wind energy projects generate revenue for local communities by providing lease payments to property owners and tax revenue to municipalities.

Energy independence : By increasing the use of wind energy, countries can reduce their dependence on imported fossil fuels and increase their energy independence.

Innovation engine : The development of wind energy technologies promotes innovation and technological progress in the energy industry.

Grid stability : Wind energy can contribute to grid stability when combined with other renewable energies such as solar energy and storage technologies.

Energy efficiency : Wind turbines are becoming increasingly efficient, both in terms of energy production and the materials used to make them.

Cost reduction : The cost of installing wind turbines has fallen significantly in recent years, making wind energy more competitive.

However, integrating wind energy into the energy system also requires challenges such as grid integration, as the wind blows irregularly, as well as taking into account environmental impacts and acceptance among the population. Nevertheless, wind energy is a key component of the energy transition and plays a crucial role in the transition to a sustainable and low-carbon energy supply.

10.2 Integration of wind energy into the power grid

Integrating wind energy into the power grid is an important step towards a sustainable energy supply and reducing dependence on fossil fuels. Wind turbines generate electricity by using wind power, but the availability of wind is unpredictable and varies widely, making integration into the power grid a technical challenge. Here are some key considerations when integrating wind energy into the grid:

Grid stability: The fluctuating availability of wind energy can affect grid stability. This requires the development of strategies to predict wind energy production and the provision of reserves to compensate for grid fluctuations.

Energy storage: Integrating energy storage systems, such as batteries or pumped storage power plants, can help smooth out fluctuations in wind energy production and store the electricity generated when it is not needed for later supply to the grid.

Grid expansion: The existing power grids often have to be expanded in order to effectively integrate wind turbines into the grid. This may include the construction of new transmission lines and substations.

Forecasting and planning: Accuracy in forecasting wind energy production is critical to optimizing the operation of the electric grid. Advances in weather forecasting and wind forecast technology are important here.

Power grid flexibility: Renewable energy integration requires a flexible power grid capable of adapting to fluctuating generation. This can be achieved through the use of intelligent grid technologies and dynamic load management.

Grid services: Wind turbines can also provide grid services such as frequency regulation and voltage stability to support grid stability.

Market design: The development of electricity market regulations and incentives can promote the integration of renewable energy and encourage investment in wind turbines.

Environmental impacts: When integrating wind energy, environmental impacts must also be taken into account, particularly in relation to bird and bat conservation and landscaping.

The integration of wind energy into the electricity grid therefore requires careful planning, technology development and investments in the electricity infrastructure. It is an important step towards reducing greenhouse gas emissions and creating a sustainable energy future.

10.3 Challenges and possible solutions

The energy transition and the expansion of the electricity grid through wind power pose many challenges, but there are also various solutions to overcome these challenges. Here are some of the key challenges and possible solutions:

1. Volatility of wind energy:

Challenge: Wind energy production is highly dependent on the weather and is therefore irregular and volatile.

Solutions:

Expansion of the network infrastructure: A well-developed transmission network enables fluctuations in wind energy production to be balanced out by transporting excess energy from wind-rich areas to wind-poor regions.

Energy storage: The development and use of energy storage technologies such as batteries, pumped storage power plants and power-to-gas systems can help to store excess wind energy and access it again when needed.

2. Landscape and environmental impacts:

Challenge: The construction of wind turbines can have negative impacts on the landscape and wildlife.

Solutions:

Site selection: Selecting appropriate locations that have lower environmental impact is crucial. This requires careful planning and environmental impact assessments.

Technological innovations: Advances in wind power technology can help minimize environmental impacts, for example through quieter and more bird-friendly systems.

3. Network stability and integration:

Challenge: Integrating wind energy into the power grid requires careful planning to ensure grid stability.

Solutions:

Smart Grids: The introduction of intelligent power grids (smart grids) enables better control and monitoring of electricity flow to ensure grid stability.

Forecasting and flexibility: Improved weather forecasts and flexible power generation, for example through gas or hydroelectric power plants, can help offset fluctuations in wind energy production.

4. Acceptance among the population:

Challenge: The construction of wind turbines is sometimes met with resistance from the public due to concerns about noise, landscape changes and health risks.

Solutions:

Citizen participation: Involving the population in decision-making processes and the opportunity to participate financially in wind projects can increase acceptance.

Transparent communication: Communication about the benefits of wind energy, the environmental impact and the measures to minimize disruption is crucial.

5. Costs and Competitiveness:

Challenge: The expansion of wind power can require high initial investments.

Solutions:

Funds and incentives: Governments can provide financial incentives and support programs for the expansion of renewable energy, including wind power, to reduce costs.

Economies of scale: As production increases and technology improves, the cost of wind turbines will tend to decrease.

Addressing these challenges requires a holistic approach that takes into account technology, infrastructure, policies and public acceptance. Wind power can play an important role in

the transition to clean and sustainable energy if these
challenges are successfully met.

Chapter 11: The Future of Wind Power

11.1 Potential for future growth

The potential for future growth in wind power is significant in many parts of the world. Wind power has become an important renewable energy source in recent decades, helping to reduce greenhouse gas emissions and diversify energy supplies. Here are some of the key factors affecting the potential for future growth in wind power:

Technological Advances : Wind power technology has continued to advance, resulting in more efficient wind turbines and lower costs. Advances in blade design, transmission technology and materials science could further increase efficiency and increase profitability.

Cost Reductions : The cost of installing wind turbines has fallen significantly in recent years, making wind energy more competitive. This trend is expected to continue as economies of scale, improved technologies and competition continue to reduce costs.

Policy support : Many countries have taken policy measures to promote renewable energy and advance the expansion of wind power. This policy support can stimulate the growth of the industry.

Climate targets : Achieving the climate targets under the Paris Agreement requires significant reductions in greenhouse gas emissions. Wind power can make a significant contribution to achieving these goals as it represents a low-carbon energy source.

Location advantages : Wind turbines are often built in areas with strong and stable winds. Regions with favorable wind conditions have particularly high potential for the expansion of wind energy.

Energy demand : The demand for energy is constantly increasing worldwide, and wind power can help meet this demand in a sustainable way.

Energy infrastructure : The expansion of transmission lines and networks can facilitate the integration of wind turbines into the power grid and increase the potential for renewable energy.

Storage technologies : The development of energy storage technologies such as batteries can help offset the fluctuations in electricity production from wind turbines and improve the reliability of energy supplies.

Innovative projects : There are innovative projects such as offshore wind farms and floating wind turbines that enable the development of wind energy in areas where conventional onshore systems are not possible.

Citizen participation : Involving the community in the planning and implementation of wind energy projects can increase acceptance and increase the potential for growth in many regions.

Overall, there are a variety of factors that influence the potential for future growth in wind power. Wind energy is expected to play an important role in the transition to a more sustainable energy supply, helping to meet global energy needs and combat climate change.

11.2 Innovations and research perspectives

Innovations and research perspectives in wind power play a crucial role in the further development of this sustainable energy source. Here are some key trends and research areas in wind energy:

Greater turbine efficiency : The development of more powerful wind turbines is a major area of research. This includes improving rotor blade designs, gear systems and generator technologies to increase energy yield per turbine.

Offshore wind energy : Wind power on the high seas (offshore wind) is becoming increasingly important because the wind speeds there are more constant and higher. Research focuses on reducing installation and maintenance costs of offshore turbines, as well as more environmentally friendly foundation methods.

Intelligent control systems : Advances in artificial intelligence and data analysis enable wind turbines and wind farms to be controlled more intelligently. This helps increase efficiency and reduce downtime.

Material Innovations : Lighter and more durable materials are being explored to reduce turbine weight and cost. This can make wind turbine manufacturing and installation more economical.

Energy Conversion and Storage : Research focuses on developing more efficient inverters and energy storage solutions to balance the intermittent nature of wind energy and ensure continuous power supply.

Wind forecasting and optimization : Advances in weather forecast models and big data analytics enable more accurate wind forecasts, which can optimize wind farm planning and operations.

Bird protection : Protecting birds and bats from collisions with wind turbines is an important area of research. This includes the development of bird detection and deterrent technologies.

Hybrid energy systems : The integration of wind energy with other renewable energies such as solar and storage technologies is being explored to improve the stability of the power grid and ensure a reliable energy supply.

Recycling and sustainability : Researchers are working to extend the lifespan of wind turbines and better recycle materials to reduce environmental impact.

Community and citizen wind farms : It examines how citizens can be more involved in wind energy projects in order to increase acceptance and support for renewable energy in society.

These research perspectives are crucial to making wind power more efficient, cost-effective and environmentally friendly and to establish it as an important contribution to the global energy transition. New technologies and insights will continue to help expand wind energy as a leading renewable energy source.

11.3 Sustainability and social responsibility

The sustainability and social responsibility of wind power play an important role in the assessment and operation of wind energy projects. Here are some aspects to consider:

Environmental Impact : Wind energy is generally considered an environmentally friendly energy source because it produces significantly lower greenhouse gas emissions compared to fossil fuels. However, wind turbines can also have environmental impacts, such as affecting bird and bat populations and changing the landscape. Sustainable wind power projects must therefore carry out careful environmental impact assessments and take measures to minimize negative impacts.

Recycling and disposal : The materials used to make wind turbines should be recyclable. Proper disposal of wind turbines at the end of their life is also important to minimize environmental impact.

Resource Consumption : Manufacturing wind turbines requires resources such as steel and concrete. It is important to ensure that the extraction of these resources is sustainable and consumption is minimized.

Social acceptance : The construction of wind turbines can be met with resistance in communities. Social responsibility means taking residents' concerns seriously, including them in the planning process and offering compensatory measures if necessary.

Jobs and Economy : The wind power industry can create jobs and boost local economies. Sustainable projects should aim to employ local workers and promote value creation in the region.

Education and research : Promoting education and research in the field of renewable energy, especially wind power, is an important aspect of social responsibility. This can help develop new technologies and strengthen local talent.

Combating energy poverty : Wind energy can help increase access to clean energy in regions that previously lacked reliable access to it. This can be part of the social responsibility of wind energy projects.

Transparency and communication : Sustainable wind power projects should be transparent and promote communication with the public, stakeholders and local communities. This creates trust and enables open dialogue.

The sustainability and social responsibility of wind power are closely linked and must be in harmony to ensure long-term positive effects on the environment and society. This requires careful planning, consideration of local concerns, and a willingness to adapt and improve projects over time.

Conclusion

12.1 Summary of key findings

The discussion about wind turbines has brought forth many aspects and arguments. Here is a summary of the key findings:

Renewable energy source : Wind turbines are an important renewable energy source that helps reduce dependence on fossil fuels and combat climate change.

Environmental impacts : Although wind turbines are more environmentally friendly compared to fossil fuels, they still have impacts on the environment, including bird and bat deaths and landscape changes.

Energy efficiency : Wind turbines are efficient in producing energy because they do not require continuous fuel supplies and produce clean energy.

Jobs and Economy : The wind energy industry creates jobs and strengthens local economies, particularly in rural areas.

Noise pollution : Wind turbines produce noise that some residents find annoying. This can lead to conflicts.

Resource availability : The effectiveness of wind turbines depends on the availability of wind resources at a location.

Energy storage : The intermittent nature of wind energy requires investment in energy storage solutions to ensure continuous power supply.

Community acceptance : The acceptance of wind turbines varies greatly from location to location and often depends on local communities and their participation.

Technological Advances : Technology in the field of wind turbines has improved, which has increased efficiency and reduced environmental impact.

Regulation and policy : Energy policy and regulation plays a critical role in encouraging or inhibiting wind power development.

Economic costs : The cost of installing wind turbines has fallen in recent years, improving the economics of this technology.

Integration into the grid : Integrating wind energy into the grid requires investment in infrastructure and the development of smart grids.

Overall, wind turbines are an important component in the fight against climate change and reducing dependence on fossil fuels. However, the discussion about their advantages and disadvantages should be carried out taking into account local conditions and environmental impacts. It is crucial to continually improve technology and policy to promote the sustainable use of wind energy.

12.2 Outlook on the role of wind power in the future

The role of wind power in the future is expected to continue to be very important as it represents a sustainable and renewable energy source. Here are some key aspects and trends that could shape the outlook for the role of wind power in the future:

Expansion of wind energy capacity : The expansion of wind turbines, both onshore and offshore, is expected to increase worldwide. This is due to the increasing demand for clean energy and advances in wind power technology.

Offshore wind energy : Offshore wind farms are gaining importance due to their potential to generate large amounts of energy while reducing visibility and noise pollution from onshore facilities. However, this requires significant investments in infrastructure.

Technological innovations : Advances in wind turbine technology, including larger turbines and more efficient blades, could increase energy output per turbine and increase the competitiveness of wind power compared to other energy sources.

Integrated energy systems : Wind turbines are expected to be increasingly integrated into integrated energy systems that also include other renewable energy sources such as solar energy and energy storage. This enables a more stable energy supply.

Cost reduction : Over time, the cost of wind energy production could continue to decline, particularly as economies of scale take hold and technologies mature.

Grid expansion and storage : Expanding the power grid and developing advanced energy storage solutions are critical to balancing fluctuations in wind energy production and ensuring a reliable power supply.

Environmental Impacts : It is expected that future wind power projects will pay increased attention to environmental impacts and the integration of environmental protection measures to minimize negative impacts on birds, bats and ecosystems.

Political support : Political support for renewable energy, including wind power, will be crucial in many countries to drive expansion. This can take the form of subsidies, incentives and regulatory measures.

Global cooperation : International cooperation and trade agreements could promote cross-border trade in wind energy and the development of cross-border offshore wind farms.

Integration into society : The acceptance of wind turbines in society will continue to be important. Comprehensive communication and community participation in the planning and implementation of wind power projects is crucial.

Overall, wind power is expected to play an important role in meeting global energy needs while supporting efforts to combat climate change. However, the exact outlook depends on various factors, including technological developments, political decisions and social acceptance.

Attachment

A. Glossary of technical terms

Here is a glossary of terms and definitions related to wind power:

Wind turbine (WEA) : A machine that converts wind energy into electrical energy. It consists of rotor blades, a generator and a tower.

Blades : The aerodynamic blades of a wind turbine that capture wind and convert it into rotational energy.

Generator : An electrical device in the wind turbine that converts the rotational energy of the rotor blades into electrical energy.

Tower : The structure on which the wind turbine is mounted and which raises the rotor to gain access to stronger winds.

Hub : The part of the wind turbine to which the rotor blades are attached and which rotates with the blades.

Wind speed : The speed of the wind, which affects the performance of a wind turbine. Measured in meters per second (m/s) or kilometers per hour (km/h).

Power Curve : A graph showing the performance of a wind turbine as a function of wind speed.

Rated power : The maximum power that a wind turbine can achieve under optimal wind conditions. Measured in kilowatts (kW) or megawatts (MW).

Wind farm : A group of wind turbines clustered at one location to produce more energy.

Wind direction : The direction from which the wind blows, which affects the orientation of the wind turbines.

Pitch system : A mechanism that allows the rotor blades to be adjusted to optimally capture the wind.

Yaw system : A mechanism that orients the wind turbine in the direction of the wind to ensure maximum wind catch.

Grid : The power grid into which the generated wind energy is fed.

Grid integration : The process by which the generated wind energy is integrated into the electrical grid.

Wind speed profile : The change in wind speed with height above ground considered in wind turbine design.

Soil roughness : The condition of the surface of the ground that affects wind speed.

Wind Energy Potential : The measure of how much wind energy is available at a particular location.

Feed-in tariff : An incentive program in which wind energy producers are financially rewarded for feeding electricity into the grid.

Regeneration : The process by which excess energy from wind turbines is fed back into the power grid.

Wind turbine life cycle : The totality of phases in the life of a wind turbine, including design, manufacture, operation and dismantling.

Repowering : The process of replacing older wind turbines with more modern and more powerful models.

Offshore wind energy : Wind turbines located in the sea.

Onshore wind energy : Wind turbines located on land.

Citizen participation : The involvement of the local community in the planning, construction and operation of wind turbines.

Environmental Impact : The impact of wind turbines on the environment, including bird strikes, scenery and noise.

This glossary is intended to help you better understand the most important terms in the field of wind power. Note that some terms may have different meanings depending on the context and region.